Valedictorian of the Bottom-Feeders

relapse & withdrawal

a chapbook of brutal honesty from the pits of hell, the fall's bottom

Valedictorian of the Bottom-Feeders

relapse & withdrawal

a chapbook of brutal honesty
from the pits of hell, the fall's bottom

conceived and transcribed by

James F. Miller II

Planet Productions
Poetry & Press
An Independant Publisher

First Edition: September 2020
Printed in the United States of America
ISBN: [978-1-7338310-6-2]

dedications and salutes

To all who have suffered and understand what lies beyond this page, may the others figure out that we do not need cages. From the highest highs and the lowest lows, this is our travesty through my experiences, thoughts, and realizations. There is hope, it resides in a choice we each must make for ourselves.

To my children with all my love, forgive me for failing you over and over and over. Understand that not all is lost nor will it ever be.

To my family, thank you for always having a hand to lend and opinions to bury me in the guilt that leads to my relapse. We live in arms reach yet stay out of reach, incapable of touch and here we go around and round. My heart is full of nothing but love for everyone. Just remember I can hear the words you are saying, just sometimes we all fall short. I was destined, but...

TABLE OF CONTENTS

I.   dedications and
        salutes 1

II.   the moment of
        impact 5

III.   the circle is
        drawn 8

IV.   Ineffectively
        Recycled 9

V.   Encaging the
        Eulogy and
        Emptiness 12

VI.   The Judgement 13

VII.   enter the silence
        of solitude...16

VIII.   a pause (a pulse) 18

IX.   forsaking formalities of fuck.............................21

X.   the meaning re-evaluated, unamended, unfiltered.............................22

XI.   oh damn 27

XII.   Reaching the End of a Hallway 28

XIII.   fade out, exit 31

XIV.   slow dropped dripping 33

XV.   Swinging Upon Thick (-headed) Branches 34

XVI.   about the poet.............................39

XVII.   about the publisher.............................40

the moment of impact

we flinch, the body tightens its clinch,
balling the hand into fist, the weight shifts.
the crashing into the surface, the tearing away,
the beginning of the unwinding, its unyielding
ache of pain, squeezing tighter, nails dig
into the cocoon of the palm. it begins
the peeling away layer by layer, deeper, further
beneath the surface to uncover the source of
the hysteria that rages behind the innocence of
children's eyes. the moment pauses in time.

the mind is weak, the hunger a bad ass beast
bitch in charge, and she demands this very
moment's full attention. eyes forward.

be lost deep inside. take a breath.
this is going to last for a few minutes,
you might as well get comfortable
inside your own skin.

the baby punching ways that shit on the morals
of fiber that consist in the formulation of
society, ideas that have long since existed
as a soggy mess made upon
her firm breast. her form flinches.

she aches to be longed.
obstructing obstacles will never grant her way.

we sit anxious for an end to this
madness, its chaos, its bliss, the happiness
of the void underlining the depth of the lie.
fasten your seatbelt. the moment of impact
will fuck your stomach up. exhale, inhale.
please do tell the do not tell tale of terrors
you have survived through somehow,
the innocence dies with these little highs,
overcoming the aftermaths of madness found
in the highest lows we have ever thought
unknowable.

we beget ignorance as a stance of position
in the inquisition of acquisition, whispers
in the shadows point fingers
inadvertently. they all stare simultaneously,
the shady sides of each face found beneath
the one they wear in public.
we are all weak
at some point.

they spoil
in the heat
like a summer romance.
the rain
is inevitable
but the height
of the emotion
intends instead blood.

Valedictorian of the Bottom Feeders

the moment becomes
intense and grasps
for that with any availability
in the moment,
of the moments lost
we commence
in the invasion of
lands foreign,
our faces smile

impulsively. imperviously
perverse bigotry besets
the beast we tame within.
until then, when
it all comes to an end
as the IMPACT presses its fingers
into the weakness of fleshes mixing
scents of pain & fear.
we all succumb in the end.
that final getting off before
finally getting off,
and leave the whole world behind.

we are such tasteless,
tasty morsels, mortal
to fault, deaf, dumb,
& blind. a miserable sigh
before a silence eternal.

exhale.
we hope you enjoyed
your flight.

the circle is drawn

is it the taste we crave
or the love of the affection
of the faces huddled around us
deep in that very moment?
does it even matter that this is
the only time they seem
to ever make an appearance?
is this a hereditary curse,
a genetical disfunction
that was placed upon our souls
in that very moment before
our placement here, this, now?
a consolation prize, that last stupid result
of the lotto numbers
we filled in on the card,
colored in the little circles
with the short, eraser-less
number two pencil.
are we fucked to
always be this pathetic?
do not blacken the glass.
do not be slow to pass.
do not stare the piece
as it shuffles around the room.
know your place, learn the rules
or lose your place
in this sacred circle,
this bullshit destruction.
this moment of disfunction.
we cannot find the will
or desire to leave. (good enough alone).

Ineffectively Recycled

a lesser man would shun his creator,
raise high his fist to the heavens above
and curse the cruelty underlying
this joke of an excuse passed off as a gift,
this oh-so-fucking-damn-glorious thing, life.

this is not a life, rather it's a purgatory.
we are waiting for the trigger to pull, waiting
for the film to reach its end
with that annoying fluttering noise that the
damn projector makes
as the lights boasted those bright ass LEDs,
and all in attendance are blind in a scene
that is as white as an angel's robe.
But not even with broken wings
nor back-alley handshakes
will any angels ever be seen here on
this barren stretch and we citizens damned to it
are forever forbidden from any outside
interference.

& like marionettes these strings are constantly
pulled to and from,
tugging with whiplashed intensity until
there is no other choice but to bow, remaining
upon the knees before the king, the creator.
giving sacrifice and thanks for the shitty day.

each time causing the heavens
to chuckle their thunderous laugh
teasing the patron in the jester's hat.
its bells jingling in silent decay,
constantly creating silent smirks, and
whispered giggles.

i am dreaming of the endless end,
in which the night finally gives birth
to, an idea so virgin the lips cannot help
but drool with ecstasy:
peace, unity, purpose.

awaiting like school children restless
in the lunch line waiting to be served
the synthetic, but almost as genuinely real as
the real deal, soybean burgers
with the new standard, twice-microwaved
macaroni, a celery stick, and past-its-prime
milk all for an unfair price.
broke, I will beg for mercy from the merciless
prick above which always ensures a shooting
pain that vines out, and suffocates me slowly
like morning glories capturing a beautiful
flowerbed.

Valedictorian of the Bottom Feeders

a lesser man would spit back into the face
& unleash upon its head his hand
with teeth tearing away the flesh, inch by inch.
these sins stain the soul like grass upon denim,
an over-worn stigma, crucifying
the innocence before it becomes
a casualty,

like a casual, conversational rape-like standard
we are created to be made to feel, to adapt
to being constricted more, yet feeling less,
as the knots tighten the rope firmly,
the throat swallows its last air.

to be called home and then blinded
such is my luck, the fucking irony
is as much a travesty as it is a tragedy
existing as the light that engulfs the masses
& overshadows the sideshow shit-stain
overcast that has become as over-worn as
re-worn daily, dirty underwear.
I am always tripping over my own feet,
awakening mid-fall from somewhere far,
its collision creating a ginormous thud
followed by a familiar beat, laughter, and
applause. as I return just in time for the
summer's circus festivities to restart.
that is just my fucking luck.

This hell is inescapable, the repetition without
definition; i await the rinse cycle.

Encaging the Eulogy and Emptiness

it became too late
to run
to hide
too pointless to hold the breath,
the onset of strobe light seizures
induced even with the eyes closed,
as the vomit formed thicker
with an enhanced heartbeat.

the entirety of life-past,
present, and forthcoming
passed before eyes so empty.
the start to the end of a cycle,
the saying goodbyes to freedom
and to the prostitutes
still there sitting with their heads
buried in your lap.

swallowing that difficult gulp
as the cold steel clicks its final clicks &
the hand presses the back of the head,
it pushes you down and into the squad car.
never again will they speak
the same of you again
for their paranoia has begun
and everyone will tell a million lies
to lessen your character
despite that you had the right to remain silent,
and your lips remained sealed tight.
none of it matters for the twists
that will be added thereon.

The Judgement

it came down like a torrential downpour
with the thunderous crash of a gavel's
pound, echoing solid the sound
of good hard oak colliding with the hickory
desk.

it is that dry gulp that rests
at the back of the throat
the inevitable saturation of suffocation,
nothing can move it or break it free,
neither can the increased heartbeat be slowed.
the sweaty palms nor the sweat dripping
from the brow & armpits cannot be
misconstrued.
this anxiety comes along with their judgment,
hand in hand as all is drunk out of the same
glass,

thereon until time's end,
the judgment will become passed with looks,
silent whispers with each word
consciously spoken by all in attendance
who will witness your shameful walk past.

it will always be a life sentence because it is life,
happening everywhere, every minute
of every day, as regrettable as it is unavoidable,
the school bullies will always be waiting
to collect the dues
they feel they are owed.

it's because before the weak become
the intelligent, wealthy, and untouchable,
they are then just the weak, and easily
intimidated,
and this day belongs to the strong and hungry.

this division begins very early in our lives.
it starts when the children are gathered
ever-so-young, piled atop one another &
forced into the jar, that bubble of necessity
called society.

this labeling advances gradually
like technology over the years.
standards are birthed from that shadows cast,
molded by the most innocent of days
eventually becoming standard programming
almost like it's a remote-control button
on the television console.

we are forever doomed in existence
to become those simple chessboard memoirs
of every victory & defeat encountered,
with each move recorded with substantial
notes accompanying
the thoroughly covered reaction times,
mannerisms and without doubt,
each strategy chosen and its path walked.
someone always strives to be able to know
every detail-
from the lights we have chosen to embrace
to what hides in the darkness from which we
cower & retreat.

Valedictorian of the Bottom Feeders

there is always someone keeping
an unspoken score that defines
but one simple outcome:
those cruel creatures we are
being molded into becoming,
those standards to which all
must and will adhere to or face the costs
of the ultimate tragedy beyond
social acceptance, becoming the outcasts.
status will be forfeited as a cost
of the punishment to be induced
for any adversities and diversities displayed
outright & openly.

despite the judge hearing the testimony,
the sentencing remains unchanged.
guilt only depends upon the choice made
and which side of the situation the judge leans,
which side of the isle has paid the larger dues,
who in the room has the dirtiest knees
from their efforts to empower those impotent
and incompetent figures so thirsty
and hungry for power and recognition;

for which side the flipped coin falls upon
after its sinister spin on its side
slowly slowing before stopping to rest.
save your breath, it is pointless to contest
your words will not be considered, and your
testimony will not be heard.

take a seat, you are here, you are guilty.

enter the silence of solitude
where did everyone go?

once a step could not be made
without tripping over a clusterfuck
of twacked-out idiots identifying
themselves as the best of friends
or misconstrued to feel the entitlement
to call themselves family.

the room is full of ghosts
only the memory and stale
scent of stagnant smoke
lingers
reminding of the smokescreen of lies
clouding the vision
of yesterday

we long to feel that acceptance
even after we learn its truth
is the root of deceit.
never will the surface be seen
and the waters beneath clear enough
to extract even a small fraction of its secrets.
the walls cannot speak
but something in the situation is off.
changed, washed, rinsed, & dried are the
sheets,
the guilt is written on all their faces

and despite the false fractions,
her pussy may feel still-so-tight
but it has never held any loyalty to anyone
except the high.
you surely are not its only exception.

we suffer in the void of information,
drown in the resulting deception,
& second guess the infection
and its infiltration.

yet the scent of bullshit descends
like the faces who pretend
and the unspoken actions they defend,
their guilt as deep as the oceans, shit.

damn it, fuck.
do not just sit there, you better wash your shit
and visit the doctor fast
or you are going to die from secrets and lies
that form the silence
everyone keeps pressed between their lips.
do not become another victim of the bullshit.

does it itch?
just wait, give it time.

a pause (a pulse)

this whole life is a madness in repetition
that will accompany me to my extinction.
there is no breaking the cycle.
just know it has never escaped my thought,
my state of mind, remaining at
the edge of my sight just out of my reach.

is this the end or just the beginning?
and just like the remedy,
either remains a trigger that itches,
begging to be pulled
all depending upon the toss of a coin,
steadily spinning on its edge,
its circumference becoming engulfed
by the endless stretch of emptiness never
imagined. time.

this is the comedown,
that raw jerk of the body,
a pure emotion
that has it shaking down to its core,
has it falling upon hurt knees.
it's funny how we cannot stand to not stand,
but how long can one fight and resist
coming down
before it becomes acceptable and amendable?

this addiction is like an ever-escaping flea
journeying across the galaxy,
stirring up the worst imaginable itch,
one that is felt from within, beneath the skin.
exhale, breathe.
just breathe, you are only weak.
do not call this relapse a defeat.
you must find your center,
balance only becomes effective
from the instability of taking a chance.

I tear away the flesh
with every stretch & contraction
of my fingertips,
and that itch spreads further out inch by inch.
I peel away the realizations
of a reality I hurt to again greet, sobriety.
I am an addict.
I will ache to remind myself I am alive
in that descending downward climb
from the happiness above the clouds.

before long, this long flight will touch down.
we count our blessings,
too few upon one hand,
each so small but feeling so large.
we will smile just as scarred eyes will dry-
the red will lessen
and we may again take control of our life.
body. mind. soul.

slowly it will take hold,
reevaluate that urge to reach a half-stretch
away.
the torment is a game of how long
can you resist the urge to stray from the
outlined course, despite knowing the ugliness
of the fate assigned to be the consequence.

temptations sing like the sirens
along the rocky coasts that
shipwrecked sailors have spoken of endlessly,
those tiny details passed as fables,
but yet we know them as our truths,
there waiting just a half stretch away.

I welcome the changing of times, faces, places,
& those forsaken formalities of fuck
for fucking the fucked mind with the fuckery of
fucking foolish fucking factions formed
without a fraction of forgiveness that refuse to
be forgotten.

I can do this. I can do this.

forsaking formalities of fuck

She speaks in riddles
everyone knows to be lies
but you hang upon each word
as if it were the divine gospel.

You hear the snickering
in the whispers spoke under their breath,
the writing on the walls
unveils the truths sought.

blind and deaf, wise yet stupid
you will idle along this course,
slowly pushing them all away
to their surprise

you will be to blame
this will always be your fault
they speak behind your back
omitting their guilt

what pieces of shit cannot own up to
their Benedict Arnold ways?
as if not speaking it
washes it all away.

fucking fuck
how can anyone tolerate
this screaming insanity in the silence,
forsaking the wake lurking
just beyond the horizon

the meaning re-evaluated, unamended, unfiltered

stop taking from this disaster
and presenting to us repeatedly
the same old lies
generationally regurgitated,
slid from the sleeve
like a card from the deck.
it cannot undo the done.
the clouds still will have come
and from them fell still this,
the black rain's reign
so painfully familiar.
its scent lingers reminiscently like a detail
specific and solid, belonging to this story.
its meaning re-evaluated,
unamended, unfiltered.

you are too late to stop
the withering and decay.
too late to reach the fading hand before fast
disappearing out of grasp, beyond reach,
and over the edge of the bottomless fall.
delivering a new birth so chilling to the bone.

we do not bury our dead
when we toss them over the deck
like horses on the crystal ship.
herded to edge, distracted,
and shoved to their death.

shake from me these feelings
I have grown so accustomed to,
so fresh each day I awaken.
the pain of the world should not seem to exist
to be all mine alone,
to feel in this smothering storm,
empathetic tears that fall like frozen bullets
rapidly discharged from reddened eyes,

blackening like the changing of seasons.
silently moving forward along their course
in this skeleton-less-like structure that stands
as ever-so-firmly as the old oak tree,
deeply rooted.
the days roll further along.
a fact needs not be a spoken notification
for the affirmation of conformity.

what a fucked generation were we
that we took this mess we were left
and like a child, reacted by stirring the pot
with our giant invisible metaphoric spoon
before we stood up,
displaying with sick satisfaction
that ginormous ear-to-ear shit-eating grin.
we walked out of the room
behind us, with courtesy, pulling shut the door
then running off outside to play.

after all, it was not our mess to begin with,
and to follow-the-leader we stick to the suite
and leave it behind, unspoken,
for someone else to deal with.

acting like there shall be no repercussion
following the footsteps of those
unaccountable,
just like our parental role model's
footprint dialect.
the pre-architectural intellect
that lacks the footing
and solidarity of sound sincerity.

just stay asleep behind the wheel
and swallow that inevitable possibility.
the time is surely coming. it is already too late
for anyone to prevent the casual casualties
existing just like calm calamities
for our wood-stained floor was etched deeply,
not just scratched gently upon the surface
as it was described to be in the advertisement
that enticed me.

those cock-sucking, stupid ass-fucking
hypocrites are probably
still there lingering, standing, arguing
pointlessly,
the behind the scenes actions not revealed to
the television audience,
you know, those distracting the attention
from attracting the response intended,
then followed by a lack of responsibility
and an explanation to solidify the reasons
for why this kind of shit keeps happening.
the hiding-in-plain-sight fuckery that could
prove that this will not be just a scuff
so easily buffed out, buried beneath the shine

Valedictorian of the Bottom Feeders

we are those pathetic few chosen,
the left behind, those stick figures
from the reality that hope will be
nothing more than this light so dim.
these tears, this flood of ever-feeling emotion
is every grain of sand in tomorrow's alien body.
a newfound world of mystery,
the story of existence
without any drawable conclusion of the
evolution,
a new beginning only so temporarily slightly
baring
any kind of light on the grinding bearings
of this crash-landing collision mishandling,
or its demolition-like unraveling story so
compelling.

yet, unbeknownst, we will be unmistakably
the scabs on the faces of a distant generation.

until again history relives itself inevitably
becoming a dying mankind, so in pain waving
without staggering their white flag
involuntarily,
unaware of the reality that for them too sadly
the roadside signs all forbid the reacting
and shun the picking up of hitchhikers in this
galaxy,
insisting instead to rather walk away
without looking back
to see them swallowed in the tragedy.
just let them burn. out.

Valedictorian of the Bottom Feeders

I shed a tear for you, my brother, my sister.
I feel every wince of your pain,
just like I am right there standing
beside you,
a new interlude.

oh damn

we cannot help
our being damaged
being damned
being drained
being dormant
broken and docile
bitter, doped up,
dosed out, undriven,
dove in, downed,
drove through, dented.
determining the density of a donut
drowned in the (absence of)
deniability of disability

those are my muffins dick

Reaching the End of a Hallway

we reach out as we break,
crumble, collapse,
fall onto the ground.
unwelcoming is that crash
landing
and the just stuck feeling
that accompanies the lying there
for countless days,
fetal position assumed
crying over an imaginary pain
that feels no less than
real.

death knocks before it bangs
upon that door.
like scared children hesitating
a deer in the headlight-like reaction,
we freeze,
stiffen, stall out at that most crucial moment.
we shrink so small hoping to be unnoticed,
even if upon fire, we would pray
to be minuscule and insignificant
to the beast searching.

foolish, our subconscious laughs
aware we cannot hide from its glory,
its moment:
death, weakness.

stay calm,
take a deep breath.

how sickening the silence becomes.
how deafening it is
-an epidemic denied its entitlement,
punishing the effect of the withdrawal.
but a name, no acknowledgement will be given
instead then choosing to believe in hope
-hoping to choose the lesser torment.

can the damned be redeemed?
what is the resale price?

like the truths, the bureaucracies
naming these bewildered bullshit policies
are put into place not to protect
us, but instead
to take in the entirety,
that wealth of white privilege
to turn a profit off
forcing further forward the extinction
of the poorer places of the lesser people.

those not chosen to be on the team
become strengthened with silence,
in the rejection embraced. the outlaws &
outcasts.

time churns, turning
the penny into all desirable things
unimaginable to the ones
not in the know,
suffering in the now,
yet these will be the criticized,
the crucified, called by name
the savages
-because what the fat wildebeests above
cannot grasp, have not understood
is our necessity to survive inside
those shadows they lob.
we outcasts will one day wise up,
rise up together against

the winds whisper
a silent prayer.
the end is nearing its cycle.
the scales are tipping back
in the favor of the lesser men
they subject themselves to refer to us as.
with pride, we accept their stigmata
and wear it as a badge,
there is a new sheriff in town bitches.

fade out, exit

reddened eyes cannot deny nor hide
the dispute or propaganda to which
has been fought to uphold yet failed & flunked.
summer school is a drag, detention hall's
destructive discipline-less disciples of dogma
all too eager to step up and to spit
down into the face of authority.
being the wave resisting the peak's glory
was a trophy worthy to be upon the mantle,
displayed.

our fossil-ish ways broken down to bow
disguising the distribution of destruction
through a damnable truth. the volumes of shit
unfit, unfound, untaxed, unedited despite
still, their existence is very well known.

we drown in the sand, the same damn sand
we are found and molded from, molded
like black-speckled sprinkled frenzies of
freedom's fuckery. bashfully we redden,
embarrassed of the disguising disgust
that rusts, slowly decaying into the disposable
dispensable, distributed factions, the fractions
that comprise the distraction, its subtraction
undeniably dimmer than days previously
delivered. the last page turns.

the cover itches to be slammed shut,
such abusive behavior displayed and
implemented upon the structured sessions

of some lesson valued by generations before.
the boredom will delete the dilemma dated,
graded, grated, browned, seasoned, raw
but considered done.
wash the hands, wash the face,
peel back the sheets, fluff the pillow
where the head will lay.
mark the calendar, successful was the day
one down, 7 years and 179 more to go.

the scene slowly fades out, and the actors step
slowly off the stage and exit.
no applause, it was a tough crowd tonight.
do not take it to heart, do not take it so hard.
no one likes anyone unless they are reveling
in their own suffering shared. have you not
noticed?

It is only about the self, worry about you
because no one else has a fuck to lend.
good game chap, good game.

slow dropped dripping

what a wasted life this madness has
transformed into being

transitioning itself as the
wildebeests in jeopardy
of the moments crucial

hearing distant laughter,
fade into the backdrop.

like flies swarming shit until there is nothing
left to
lactate your lusts elsewhere

this is not how it was meant to end

checkmate.
well played.

I was once destined, but
my mouth would not refrain
alas.

weave the rope, tie the knots, climb the stool
but there is so much work left to do

tomorrow, maybe if
destined, but...

Swinging Upon Thick (-headed) Branches

(My Jaded Family Tree)

I know my reflection does not cast
The greatest joy inside my father's heart
Nor does it inspire my family in any positive
manner.
I am all their regret and shame pressed and
copied.
I am but a dandelion, an infection
They cannot poison nor sever fast enough
To escape.

Their words, combined with their lack of
actions
 Are the only roadmap I have been given to
navigate
through this mad world, yet egos become their
voices
that ridicule my every wrong turn made,
my every pause was again taken to re-evaluate
and to find the center that I had made

the sadness is a melancholy numbing inside.
I would have swung from a branch years ago,
but even still today they would not have
noticed.
to expect that they would pause
between their harsh words
would have been too much to ask.
thus, it would have been but a death in vain.

Valedictorian of the Bottom Feeders

I spark a smile, fly a finger, and shake every
hand along the way.
I rejoice in my errors and teach others to do the
same.
I never signed up for a popularity contest,
because I was never beauty pageant material.
thus, I allow the lost to move their lips
in whatever necessary way they may require,
their sounds are the doldrums to eardrums
 accustomed to modern-day tunes.

when I reach the line and finally this day is
finished,
I will either be closer or further
lost in some fucked up way,
but despite there being no crowd in the
bleachers
cheering my name, I cannot complain.
I will still make it.
it will somehow still work.
tomorrow will be a brighter day.
I never did need that superstar welcome,
I would never have fit in to begin with.

Valedictorian of the Bottom Feeders

I accept I am trash, white, dirt, addicted, lost,
selfish
and a piece of shit too unfit to be a father
or a mentor to every or any other.
these words I have heard tapping my brain
like a summer rain against the car roof,
a white noise static that drowns the sunshine
overhead.

I would love for one day their traps
to silence this hatred they spew
and for their eyes to open
to finally see the truth in any light.
I am humble and own every flaw.
yet, you sing with the choir
and your echoes I grow to ignore

I will accept I should swing from a tree branch
but when I take that plunge will you silence
your ego
to see me swinging and the lights above
descending
or will I need to wait until you have finished
your cake
and that slice of pie that I suggested you might
enjoy too?
I served you each plate and handed you your
spoon.
I did these things with a smile to beget
how satisfying it was to grow up to be
anything but a hypocrite like you.

Valedictorian of the Bottom Feeders

about the poet

James F. Miller II is a poet who hails from the Midwestern United States. He attended several universities and studied a wide range of majors before leaving the educational world to seek out the philosophical value of life on the road and pursuits of dreams in the music industry. He has published two full length poetry collections, A Footnote for Tomorrow (4/2019) and Ghost in the Reflection-Letters to Erin (2/2020). (You can learn more about him and his work at a number of social media sites and at https://www.poetryofjamesfmillerii.com).

about the publisher

Planet Productions Poetry & Press was founded in 2018 and implemented to be a tool for the voices who speak in empty rooms and the ears that need to hear their message. The company is located both in Indiana and Arizona. For a list of upcoming and previous titles or for more information on how to submit poetry for publication in a chapbook or one of the ezines, visit https://www.planetproductionspoetrypress.com

You can learn more about Jim :

Twitter at: @jim_twenty https://www.twitter.com/jim_twenty

on **Facebook at:** https://www.facebook.com/poetryofjamesfmillerii

on **Instagram at:** https://www.instagram/jamesfmillerii_poet

on **Amazon Author Central at:** https://www.amazon.com/author/jamesfmillerii

his **webpage:** https://www.poetryofjamesfmillerii.com

his **Channillo series:** https://channillo.com/user/28091/

his **YouTube channel:**:
https://www.youtube.com/channel/UC3JwyUWDmK8mHdq8uOOqvUQ

on **GoodReads** at:
https://www.goodreads.com/author/show/19079818.James_F_Miller_II

You can purchase his books at:

Amazon.com

> *A Footnote for Tomorrow:* https://www.amazon.com/dp/B07Q23NJ87
> *Ghost in the Reflection-Letters to Erin:*
https://www.amazon.com/dp/B07YHK5R4W

TheBookPatch.com

> *A Footnote for Tomorrow:*
https://app.thebookpatch.com/BookStore/ghost-in-the-reflection-letters-to-erin/0c34c169-d729-450a-8104-945b65d71369?isbn=9781733831000
> *Ghost in the Reflection-Letters to Erin:*
https://app.thebookpatch.com/BookStore/a-footnote-for-tomorrow/51b0b4a5-5ceb-4a16-b372-9009e3967032?isbn=9781733831048

Poetry, Music, & More Online Retail:
https://www.planetproductionsandmore.com

Barnes and Noble: www.barnesandnoble.com/w/ghost-in-the-reflection-letters-to-erin-james-miller/1136305488
And many more online book retailers

www.ingramcontent.com/pod-product-compliance
Lightning Source LLC
Chambersburg PA
CBHW021117020426
42331CB00004B/532